LET'S-READ-AND-FIND-OUT SCIENCE®

STAGE 2
3.4

The PLANETS in Our SOLAR SYSTEM

by Franklyn M. Branley • illustrated by Kevin O'Malley

HarperCollinsPublishers

Special thanks to Jurrie van der Woude
at NASA for his expert advice.

The *Let's-Read-and-Find-Out Science* book series was originated by Dr. Franklyn M. Branley, Astronomer Emeritus and former Chairman of the American Museum–Hayden Planetarium, and was formerly co-edited by him and Dr. Roma Gans, Professor Emeritus of Childhood Education, Teachers College, Columbia University. Text and illustrations for each of the books in the series are checked for accuracy by an expert in the relevant field. For more information about Let's-Read-and-Find-Out Science books, write to HarperCollins Children's Books, 10 East 53rd Street, New York, NY 10022, or visit our web site at http://www.harperchildrens.com.

Library of Congress Cataloging-in-Publication Data
Branley, Franklyn Mansfield, date
    The planets in our solar system / by Franklyn M. Branley ; illustrated by Kevin O'Malley.
       p.   cm. — (Let's-read-and-find-out science.   Stage 2)
    Summary: Describes the nine planets and other bodies of the solar system; includes directions for making models showing the size of the planets and their distance from the sun.
    ISBN 0-06-027769-6. — ISBN 0-06-027770-X (lib. bdg.). — ISBN 0-06-445178-X (pbk.)
    1. Planets—Juvenile literature.   2. Solar system—Juvenile literature.   [1. Planets.   2. Solar system.]
I. O'Malley, Kevin, date, ill.   II. Title.   III. Series.
QB602.B73   1998   97-1174
523.4—dc21   CIP
                                                                                                        AC

Typography by Elynn Cohen
11   12   13   14   15   16   17   18   19   20
❖

The PLANETS in Our SOLAR SYSTEM

4

We all live on a planet.
Our planet is called Earth.
It is one of nine planets that
go around the sun.

MERCURY

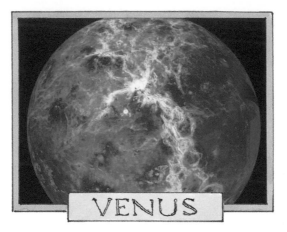

VENUS

EARTH

URANUS

NEPTUNE

PLUTO

MARS

JUPITER

SATURN

You probably know the names of some of the planets. Maybe you know all of them. The nine planets are Mercury, Venus, Earth, Mars, Jupiter, Saturn, Uranus, Neptune, and Pluto.

The nine planets are part of the solar system.

The most important part of the solar system is the sun. The word *sol* means sun in Latin. So the solar system means "the sun system."

After the sun, the most important parts of the solar system are the nine planets.

Have you ever tried to find the planets in the sky?
Uranus, Neptune, and Pluto are very dim. You need
a telescope to see them.

You don't need a telescope to see Venus, Mars, Jupiter, or Saturn. They look like bright stars, but they don't twinkle. They glow. You may have seen them and thought they were stars.

You don't need a telescope to see Mercury, either. You can see it in early evening just after sunset. The sky is not very dark then, so you have to be a good sky watcher to find Mercury.

But there is another part of the solar system that you can see easily. It is the moon. The moon goes around Earth. It's called Earth's satellite. Most of the other planets also have satellites.

Asteroids are also part of the solar system. So are comets and meteoroids. Asteroids are big chunks of rock that go around the sun. Many are as big as a house. Some are as big as a mountain, or even bigger.

Comets are collections of ice, gas, and dust. The center of a comet may be only a few miles across. The tail of gasses may be millions of miles long.

Meteoroids are bits of rock and metal. Some are as large as boulders, but most are as small as grains of sand. Have you ever seen a shooting star? It was not really a star. It was a meteoroid falling toward Earth.

Captions for page 15
1 Asteroid 243 Ida was photographed by the Galileo spacecraft in 1993. It appears to be 32 miles long.
2 The Hale-Bopp Comet could be seen for several months in the spring of 1997.
3 This Mars meteorite was found in the ice fields of Antarctica and is 4.5 billion years old.

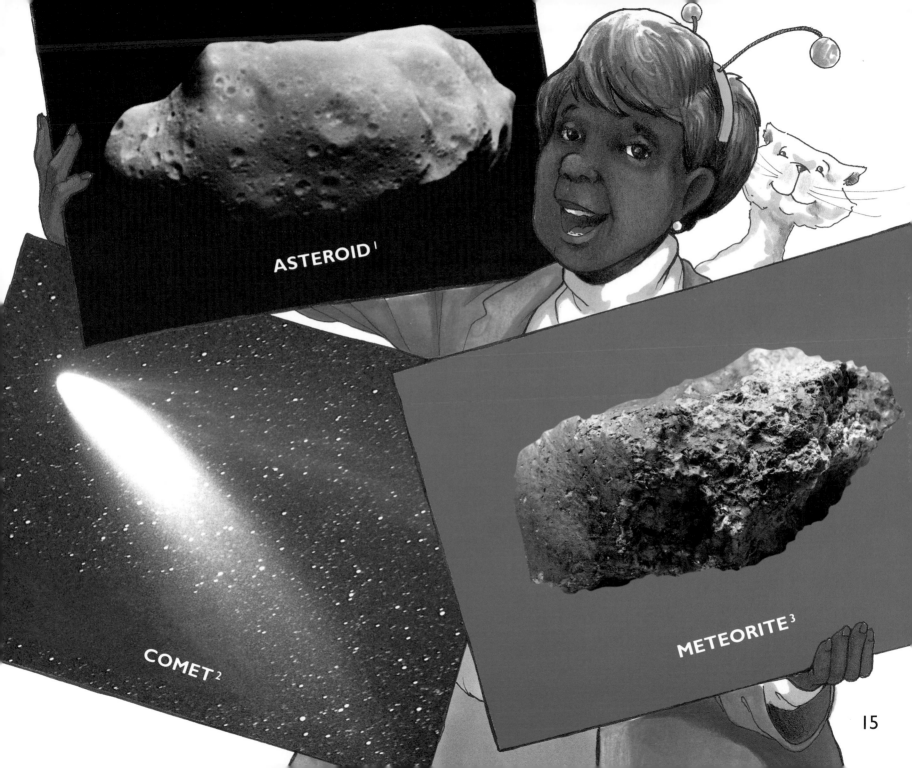

ASTEROID[1]

COMET[2]

METEORITE[3]

15

The solar system has many parts—the sun, the nine planets, the satellites of the planets, asteroids, comets, and meteoroids. The main parts are the sun and nine planets.

Seven of the planets have one or more satellites. Four of them have rings.

The nine planets move around the sun. They move in paths called orbits. The drawing shows the orbits.

Mercury takes only 88 days to go once around the sun.

Pluto takes much longer than that. It takes about 248 years.

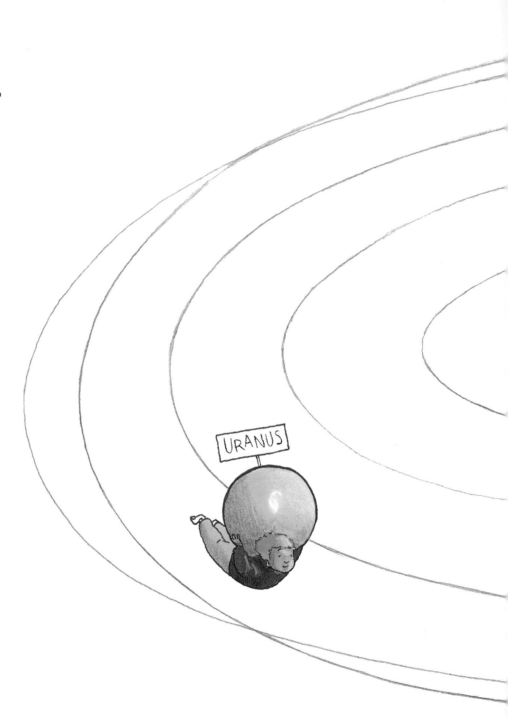

URANUS

Mercury is closer to the sun than any other planet, but even Mercury is millions of miles from the sun.

Suppose you could fly from Mercury to the sun in a rocket. And suppose the rocket went 50,000 miles an hour. It would take more than four weeks to get there.

It would take the same rocket over eight years to go from Pluto to the sun.

Pluto is farther from the sun than any other planet, but it isn't always. From 1979 to 1999 it has been closer to the sun than Neptune. From 1999 to 2250 Pluto will once more be the farthest planet from the sun.

Neptune and Pluto are farthest from the sun. That is why they are the coldest planets. Temperatures on these planets are about 328°F below zero.

That's much colder than any place on Earth. Even the South Pole never gets that cold.

PLUTO

Mercury and Venus are the hottest planets. The temperature on Mercury reaches 600°F. Sometimes it is much colder. On Venus the temperature stays around 860°F.

Plants and animals cannot live on Mercury or Venus. They would burn up. They cannot live on Neptune or Pluto either. They would freeze. Jupiter and Saturn are also very cold.

Of all the planets, Earth is the only one where people live. We think no other planet in our solar system has plants or animals of any kind. Earth is the "life planet."

Earth is a middle-sized planet. Four of the planets are smaller than Earth. They are Mercury, Venus, Mars, and Pluto. Four of the planets are larger than Earth. They are Jupiter, Saturn, Uranus, and Neptune.

Jupiter is the biggest of all the planets.

It is much bigger than Earth. Suppose Jupiter were a large, hollow ball. Over 1,000 Earths could fit inside it.

Pluto is the smallest planet. It is much smaller than Earth. It is even smaller than the moon. More than 100,000 Plutos would fit inside Jupiter.

Earth is the most important planet to you, and to all of us. That's because it's the planet where we live. It is not the biggest planet in the solar system, nor is it the smallest. It is not the hottest or the coldest. Earth is about in the middle. And it's just right for us.

SOLAR SYSTEM MOBILE

You can make a mobile of the solar system that will show the differences in the sizes of the planets. You will need:

cardboard	markers or crayons	5 small twigs or
compass	string	wooden rods
pencil	tape or glue	

Using the table below as a guide, take your compass and trace circles to represent the planets. Then cut them out of cardboard and color them (see pages 6–7 for reference). Jupiter and Saturn will be very big.

Mercury ⅜"	Mars ⁹⁄₁₆"	Uranus 4"
Venus ⅞"	Jupiter 11"	Neptune 3 ¾"
Earth 1"	Saturn 10"	Pluto ¼"

Tape or glue a thread or light string about four or five inches long to each planet.

Gather five small twigs. They don't have to be the same length.

Tie the string from Jupiter to one end of a twig. Tie another planet—any one of them—to the other end of the twig. You can tape the strings in place if you want to.

Lay the twig across your finger. Move it from side to side until it balances. Mark that place. This is the balance point.

Tie a string around the mark. The planets should balance. If they don't, move the string until they do. Tape the string in place.

Fasten the other planets to twigs in the same manner.

One of the twigs will have only one planet, but that's all right. If the planet is a little one, the stick will still balance on your finger.

Tie the string from each twig to the balance point of another twig. All the twigs together make a mobile.

If your mobile does not balance evenly, try moving the strings a little. Or you can hang small cardboard strips on the lighter sides of the twigs. They add weight.

PLANETARY DISTANCE ACTIVITY

This model shows how far the planets are from the sun. To make this model, you'll need a long wall, thumbtacks or tape, crayons or markers, scissors, a ruler, and several sheets of paper.

Draw a picture of the sun and each planet. Color and label the drawings. Read the table to see how far from the sun each planet should be. Pick a point on the wall to be the sun and tack up your drawing. Use the ruler to measure, then put the planets where they belong.

Distances of the Planets from the Sun

Planet	Distance	Model scale
Mercury	35,898,000 miles	(2 inches in your model)
Venus	67,084,000 miles	(3 inches in your model)
Earth	92,752,000 miles	(4 inches in your model)
Mars	141,298,000 miles	(6 inches in your model)
Jupiter	482,546,000 miles	(1 foot, 9 inches in your model)
Saturn	884,740,000 miles	(3 feet, 2 inches in your model)
Uranus	1,779,152,000 miles	(6 feet, 5 inches in your model)
Neptune	2,787,892,000 miles	(10 feet, 1 inch in your model)
Pluto	3,658,000,000 miles	(13 feet, 3 inches in your model)

Neptune

Pluto

FIND OUT MORE ABOUT OUR SOLAR SYSTEM

- Plan a moon or planet vacation! What would you need to take if your family decided to visit the moon for a week? Would your supplies be different if you were to visit Saturn or Jupiter? Keep a diary of what might happen on your trip.

- It's fun to watch a full moon rise from inside your house. Find a window that lets you see the moon clearly. Cut out five or six small white circles. When you see the moon, ask a parent to tape the first circle onto the window to show where the moon was at first, and then to mark where the moon is every hour after you've gone to bed. In the morning you'll have a map of the moon's path across the sky!

- Watch the moon for a full cycle, just under a month. Each night draw a picture of the moon on a separate index card. When the cycle is over, staple the cards together in order, to make a flip book that shows the phases of the moon.

- Watch how a stick makes shadows that change throughout the day. On a sidewalk or patio put a stick in a lump of clay so that the stick stands up straight. Place the "shadow caster" in a place where it will be in the sun all day. With chalk trace the shadow that you see in early morning. Every hour or so repeat your tracing. You will see that the shadow has moved as Earth rotates. At the end of the day, join the tips of the shadows with a line. You'll have a path to show how the shadow changed.

- Visit the following web sites for photos and facts about the planets:
  http://pds.jpl.nasa.gov/planets/welcome.htm
  http://www.seds.org/nineplanets/nineplanets/nineplanets.html
  http://www.jpl.nasa.gov/